The Solar System
from 1 to

carla baredes · ileana lotersztain
translated by silvana goldemberg

El sistema solar del 1 al 10 by Carla Baredes and Ileana Lotersztain.
Original edition ©2007 ediciones iamiqué, http://www.iamiqué.com.ar

English translation copyright © 2016 by Doubledutch Books
First published in English in Canada and the USA in 2016 by Doubledutch Books

Thanks to Scott Young at the Manitoba Museum Planetarium for his critical review.
Printed in Canada

Library and Archives Canada Cataloguing in Publication
Baredes, Carla
[Sistema solar del 1 al 10. English]
    The solar system from 1 to 10 / Carla Baredes and Ileana
Lotersztain ; translated by Silvana Goldemberg.

(Science for counting)
Translation of: El sistema solar del 1 al 10.
ISBN 978-0-9940570-9-9 (paperback)

    1. Counting--Juvenile literature. 2. Solar system--Juvenile literature.
I. Lotersztain, Ileana, author II. Title. III. Title: Sistema solar del 1 al 10.
English.

QA113.B37 2016   j513.2'11   C2016-902717-1

Doubledutch Books
1427 Somerville Ave.,
Winnipeg, MB
Canada R3T 1C3

www.doubledutchbooks.com

Numbers are everywhere: in the days of school that remain until the holiday break, in the distance that separates your house from your best friend's, in the coins you have to save to buy a chocolate bar, in the number of candles you will blow out on your next birthday, in the number of bites left until you finish your dinner, and… **in the Solar System, too!**

Would you like to learn more about them?

1 star called Sun

that keeps all members of the Solar System spinning around it.

Even if you think the Sun deserves to be in a special category, **the Sun is just another star** among the trillions of stars that are in the Universe. The reason you see the Sun so big and so bright is because it is much closer to Earth than the other stars.

Just like other stars, the Sun is a huge ball of very, very, very hot gases that give off heat and light. If it were not for the heat and the light we receive from the Sun, Earth would be a dark, cold, and lifeless planet.

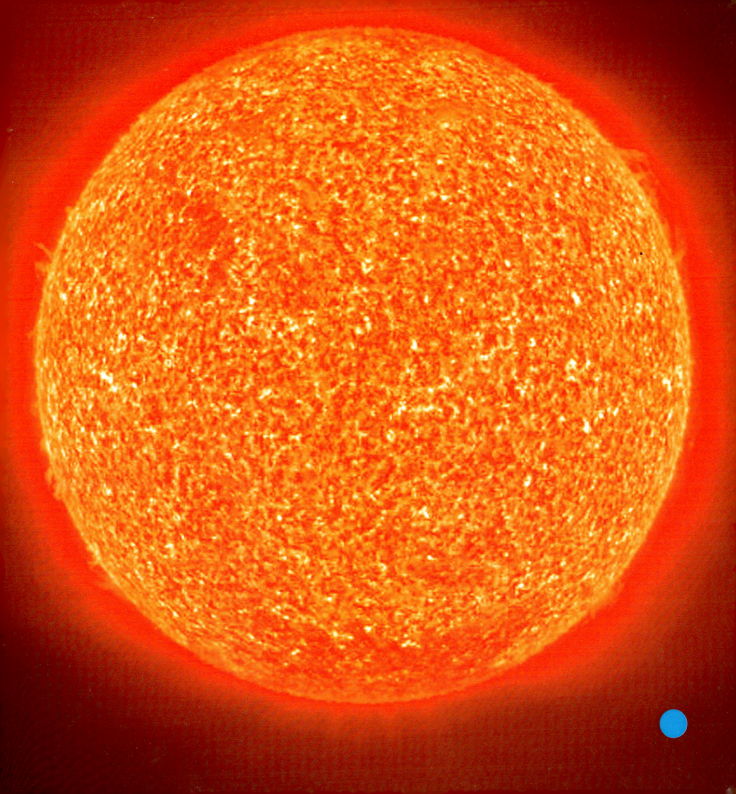

2 groups of planets separated by 1 asteroid belt

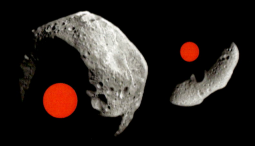

Asteroids are chunks of rock and metal that revolve around the Sun. Some are really big, although not big enough to be considered planets. Most asteroids move between Mars and Jupiter. They make up a **belt** that divides the planets into two groups: **the inner planets**, which are closer to the Sun and are quite dense, and **the outer planets**, which are true gas giants.

Asteroids are called "minor planets" because they look like planets and moons.

3 types of meteorites fall to Earth

– iron, stony, and stony-iron.

From time to time, some asteroids crash into one another and break into many pieces that scatter out in all directions. If a piece travels toward Earth, the air rubs and heats it up, in much the same way your hands get warm when you rub them. If the piece is no bigger than a pebble, it disintegrates in a flash of light before touching the ground.

We call it a **shooting star!** Have you ever seen one traveling across the sky at night? If the fragment is a little bigger and does not break down, it hits the ground. We call it a **meteorite!** If the fragment is even bigger, then it is no longer considered a meteorite, but an **asteroid.** If an asteroid hits the surface of Earth, some really amazing things can happen...like the extinction of the dinosaurs!

Barringer Crater (Arizona, USA) was formed about 50,000 years ago by the impact of an asteroid. The hole is so big that about 100 soccer fields can fit in it.

The word *meteor* comes from the Greek word *meteoros*, which means "high in the air."

4 moons

Galileo discovered around Jupiter

– Io, Europa, Ganymede, and Callisto.

About 400 years ago, the scientist **Galileo Galilei** pointed the telescope he built toward Jupiter. After much observation, he discovered Jupiter was not alone: **it had 4 moons.** This discovery was very, very important because it showed Earth is not the centre of the Universe, like almost everyone believed at the time.

Today, we know many planets have moons (also called "satellites"). In fact, most planets have more than one. Jupiter has many more moons than the 4 Galileo saw! Just as the planets accompany the Sun along its journey through the Universe, the moons accompany the planets on their journey around the Sun.

The word *satellite* comes from the Latin word *satelles*, which means "fellow traveler."

 parts to a comet

– nucleus, coma, dust tail, ion tail, and hydrogen envelope.

When a comet is very, very far from the Sun, it is like **a dirty snowball**. As it approaches the Sun, however, it gets hotter and hotter, and its appearance changes a lot. **A cloud of vapor and dust** forms around the comet and reflects sunlight, making the comet look like a shiny, fuzzy ball. In addition, some of the dust is left behind, forming **two tails**, the **dust tail** and the **ion tail**. The tails appear as the comet approaches the Sun. With each orbit around the Sun, comets become smaller. That is why it is said that comets have a short life...even if we are talking about several million years!

The word *comet* comes from the Greek word *kome*, which means "long-haired."

# Moon landings

during the missions of Apollo 11, Apollo 12, Apollo 14, Apollo 15, Apollo 16, and Apollo 17.

On July 20, 1969, half a billion people sat in front of their TVs to watch a man make history. His name was Neil Armstrong, and he was **the first human to set foot on a place beyond Earth.** As people stared in amazement, he stepped onto the Moon and said: "That's one small step for a man, one giant leap for mankind." Neil and his partner, Buzz Aldrin, spent 2 hours and 30 minutes walking on the Moon, while Michael Collins waited for them aboard the spaceship *Columbia*. The 3 of them landed back on Earth 8 days after their launch to the moon – healthy, safe, and ecstatic. After Apollo 11, there were 5 more sucessful missions to the Moon. The last one was in 1972.

Among the ancient Greeks, Apollo was the god of light, music, and poetry.

7 main rings around Saturn

and their names are anything but original: A, B, C, D, E, F, and G.

6- Saturn is the planet with the most rings and the only one that could float in the water.

8- Neptune is the farthest, the coldest planet, it has the strongest winds, and takes the longest to revolve around the Sun.

5- Jupiter is the largest and the heaviest planet, and it has the most satellites. It also has a giant storm known as the "Great Red Spot." The spot looks like a hurricane.

7- Uranus was the first planet to be discovered with the help of a telescope.

The word *planet* comes from the Greek word *planetes*, meaning "wanderer or vagabond."

9 astronauts aboard the space station ISS

on July 28, 2005.

2 were about to return to Earth: John Phillips and Sergei Krikalev; 7 had just arrived from Earth: Steve Robinson, Soichi Noguchi, Wendy Lawrence, James Kelly, Andy Thomas, Eileen Collins, and Charles Camarda.

A space station is a laboratory that revolves around Earth, a little beyond the layer of air that surrounds our planet. While at the space station, the astronauts make observations that allow us to know more about Earth and space. They also do experiments that help improve all of our lives. The ISS has been in orbit since 1998. It completes a rotation around Earth every hour and a half. Can you imagine how many orbits it has made so far? Thanks to the ISS, there have been people in space continuously since 2000. It has hosted not only astronauts, but space tourists have visited it, too. Would you like to sign up to be a visitor to the space station?

ISS is an acronym for International Space Station.

10 kilograms –
The weight of the *Sojourner* rover

Although no one has yet set foot on **Mars**, some **robots** have roamed its surface as true interplanetary travelers. The first, called *Sojourner,* reached Mars in 1997 aboard a rocket on the Mars Pathfinder mission.

Sojourner was a small, lightweight vehicle, the size of a go-kart. Its job was to take photographs of everything it found in its path while studying the soil, the rocks, and the Martian air. *Sojourner* sent valuable data back to Earth – much more than scientists expected to get. After three months, contact with it was lost forever.